Addictive Nature
By the Author Lina M. of Beyond Woman

Beyond Woman Pty Ltd
PO Box 1018
Sanctuary Cove, Qld, 4212
Australia

Copyright © 2018 Royal Diadem Publishing House Pty Ltd
                  Beyond Woman Pty Ltd
                  Lina M.

First Edition printed January 2018

Created and designed in Australia.

Scripture taken from the Holy Bible, New International Version®. Copyright © 1973, 1978, 1984, 2011 by International Bible Society.
Used by permission of Zondervan Publishing House. All rights reserved. Italics in Scripture references are for emphasis only.

Beyond Woman is a trademark of Beyond Woman Pty Ltd.

All rights reserved.

Addictive Nature
Free Yourself

By Lina

ROYAL DIADEM
PUBLISHING
HOUSE

PO Box 1018
Sanctuary Cove Qld 4212
Australia
Email: seek@royalpublisher.com

National Library of Australia Cataloguing-in-Publication entry

Creator: M., Lina, author.

Title: Addictive nature : free yourself / Lina M.

ISBN: 9780994179081 (paperback)

Subjects: Compulsive behavior.

Self-help techniques.

Life skills

Description

Addiction can be used for your strength once you are free from its grip by the power of the spirit enabling you.

Concentrate on that which is good to walk in the victory given you, and be free from the old life of seduction by moving the boundary line of restriction.

Escape the grip holding you captive.

The will to survive is not found in compromise, but in the will to remove yourself from the addiction serving to harm you. So be the willing party to free yourself like a bird and submit to freedom, rather than being enslaved to addiction ruling over you.

Your freedom depends on you and the will to survive is found in the victory given you. Free yourself and be one with your spirit supporting you.

Guide

1	Free Yourself	11
2	Evolve	13
3	Be Released	15
4	Give Not Compromise	17
5	Be Not Burdened	19
6	Give Up	21
7	The Fowler is Misleading	23
8	Enjoy Life Instead	25
9	Respond Not to Temptation	27
10	Waver Not in Faith	29
11	Be Not Ensnared	31
12	Addiction is Not of You	33
13	Grow Strong	35
14	Climb Higher	39

Guide

15	Be Anchored	41
16	Disrupt Not	43
17	Injure Not Yourself	45
18	Be Set Free	47
19	Believe in Yourself	49
20	Grow Strong	51
21	You Are Empowered	53
22	Be Encouraged	55
23	Be Renewed	57
24	Be Lifted Up	59
25	Joy In Freedom	61
26	Agony Gone	63
27	Benefit Thy Self	65

To You My Friends

You are Free

Free

From Addiction

Free Yourself

Your addiction is not your own; it belongs to another. You are a victim of choice.

Murmur no longer, for you are free from this addiction suppressing your mind and not allowing you to think clearly.

Addiction is not an obsession but a crime - hurting your body, soul and spirit.

Be released from the snare oppressing you.

You have suffered much and there is no need for you to be oppressed any longer by circumstances weighing you down.

I am the Alpha of your life and the Healer of your spirit.

Love you forever, O my child of freedom. Look to me and be free.

You are honored in my sight.

2

Evolve

I am sustained and no longer burdened by trouble from this addiction suppressing me.

I am forever thankful to heaven for saving me from the snare of addiction torturing my spirit, robbing my mind by affliction.

I am burdened by trouble and desire to be set free from past struggles - addictive situations seducing me.

I am not small-minded nor little, but feel dead, consumed by the fire of hell torturing my soul in all these situations tormenting me.

Empower yourself, child, empower yourself by my Will of love to survive these addictions blaming you.

Flee from corruption accusing you falsely.

Destroy not your memory of who you really are to Me - Love.

3

Be Released

Train yourself to quit smoking. Pay attention to your health before the season of change comes and you fade away to nothing. I am the One holding you. Grow strong and never be weakened. Give not into those desires harming your mind, disrupting your thoughts; for anything else contrary to the truth is defying.

You are to maintain self-control, for without it you are demolished, ruined, overlooked and unprotected from all sorts of negative thoughts opposing you.

The weapon of your warfare should be Love. Maintain love and never look back to old habits suppressing you. The purpose of your existence is to make a difference by living the example life. Everyone needs to see my love in action, not just with words and false humility.

Be strong and maintain the *will* to act on that which is best for you.

4

Give Not Compromise

Support me from addiction, Oh, my Deliverer; support me and remove this addiction burdening my soul. I am tortured in spirit and robbed of any hope to trust in you to save me. Comfort me, O comfort me, before the night falls and the sun rises no more. Keep me safe in the shelter of your tabernacle on every occasion.

You are not bound but free, O child, so soar the mountaintop with joy and great assurance. I am right here with you supporting you, holding your hand walking you through the deepest darkness. Look to me and you will find the answers you are seeking. Walk in the Truth you know and be relieved from stress and addictions. The key is love-- love yourself first and walk in the freedom supporting you. The power has been given into your hands.

Rule over your addiction of sorrow and do not give it a foothold.

5

Be Not Burdened

I am your Anchor of Hope to free you from all these addictions tormenting your soul, body and mind.

Acknowledge faith and faith shall free you. Walk with wisdom and wisdom shall instruct you. Walk in Love and love shall empower you. Walk with God and God shall defend you.

Move mountains if you will, but not without my strength. Every mountain hovering over your life must be removed by crushing down the strongholds suppressing you.

Recover your strength by my Will to survive these seductions inviting you to surrender. Your Alpha will help you start and your Omega will put an end to it all.

You are strong enough. Play not with the fire of addiction.

6

Give Up

Recall the days of early beginnings and never tire of doing good to all who ask you.

Keep safe from tormenting addictions that destroy the body and ruin the mind.

Comfort your heart to free yourself. You can do it - depend on me, for I can be your All.

The Anchor of Hope is your Deliverer - ask of Me to set you free.

Restrain from these addictions that are wearing you out and causing injury to your eyesight - dimming the light. Why walk in darkness when you have the Light within you?

You are my beloved, my precious child, whom I have chosen. Restrict not yourself from being free.

I am on your side. Be encouraged, get up and walk on.

7

The Fowler is Misleading

Rest your weary heart and comfort your soul during time of trouble and desertion.

My favor upon your life has given you victory.

Enjoy the ride home with me, free from any restriction and false cravings that lead you astray by the hand of the enemy.

Renew your mind to be transformed into my likeness.

Restrictive forces are holding you back from Me - your Creator. Destroy sin in the flesh and move on. Do not lie to yourself any longer.

This seduction of false pleasure is deadly - give not into it.

I am near, call on me. I am the One, who takes you places, not your addiction appearing real.

Seduction is not of me - control yourself.

8

Enjoy Life Instead

Injure not yourself by these tormenting times of trouble causing confusion. Restrain from addictions that waylay your life - enticing your soul with temptations that ruin kings. Keep safe no matter how the journey of your life may seem. Lean not on your own understanding - come away with me instead.

I have empowered you by my sufficient grace. Delight yourself with my power of grace sustaining you and my willingness supporting you. Be resurrected from your addiction holding you back from moving forward and rescue yourself quickly.

I am here, just pray to me. Ask and you shall receive. Only when I hear your voice will I answer. Healing will surely come if you look for it - ask and see. I shall empower you with determination to fight the good fight of the faith and run with the wind of my grace resting upon your shoulder to rescue you.

9

Respond Not to Temptation

Respond to temptation and you will fall.

Act on that which is best for you and you will win before the night is over, for you must struggle no longer.

There is a new day ahead - partake of my glory. Keep climbing without any hesitation or thought of what tomorrow may bring you.

I, the great Deliverer am here with you. I shall remove these huge mountains of addictions suppressing you and release you to walk the streets freely before the crowd.

This is all vanity, suppression and oppression - keep clear from it all. These trials are causing collusion in the spirit realm as well as producing negative thoughts suppressing you.

Do not deprive yourself of anything good.

You shall lack nothing of value as you let go.

10

Waver Not in Faith

I am your burden Relief, do not waver under hard trials tormenting your soul.

Grieve for the needy and help the outcast, but do not grieve my spirit by your addictions and crime torturing your soul, hurting your spirit and destroying your life.

You are no longer to be accused falsely by corruption seducing you. Stay away by the grace given you and do not lag behind, for I your Leader and Comforter am the One who is comforting you.

Keep growing in faith - aim higher daily. I am watching over your spirit to free your mind. Have courage and resist any temptation of addiction - face it in power.

Loving you for all eternity. Your Guiding Light - The Alpha and Omega of your soul, I am.

Be assured and live a life of freedom.

11

Be Not Ensnared

Keep climbing those walls away from the valley. Soon enough you shall inherit a blessing and reach your destined Mountain height with freedom.

Keep the fire of love alive within you, for I am your Leader of freedom who comforts you from sorrow and distress. Learn to love yourself, for I am the One supporting you.

Allow your mind to be recreated and reformed by Me - your Source and Love song during the night. I, the Singer of songs, am your vitality in time of trouble, doubt, fear and confusion.

Rest in me, child, and talk about your feelings.

Let your light shine upon the world in mastery and teach others the way of victory.

Be assured - I am here eternally.

Receive me; receive Life and not injury.

12

Addiction is Not of You

Help your brother who is tortured in mind, for he will soon be changed to see the light and be able to distinguish truth from false. He is confused about your love supporting him. Comfort his heart and do not neglect him. He will soon be set free from these addictions restraining him. Comfort his soul and do not act on impulse; for it corrupts. Support and lift him up from this anxiety entangling him.

I love you both; do not murder by hate and do not strip your neighbor's wife naked by your visual encounters releasing bad energy traveling through the senses, causing disturbance in the spirit realm-- corrupting the mind; diluting the heart.

You are to remain alert to the very things around you. Be switched on and never tire of loving one another for all eternity.

Your life begins now - be set free.

13

Grow Strong

I am not the One injuring you, but your addiction. Give up before it gives up on you through misfortune, sickness, illness and or disease.

Keep not company with your addiction, for it is your enemy and not your friend.

Keep company with real people who truly care about your wellbeing, that you may both benefit and learn from experiences shared.

Close not your eyes on the things that hurt, rather free yourself like a gazelle from the hand of the hunter - rule over them quickly.

I am your comfort in time of distress and struggle. Call on me and you shall find me there - at the door of your heart, ready to support.

Tell me how you feel - express yourself to me, for I am listening.

Cont... 13

I am your director of hearts and will not allow you to fall nor come to destruction by those forces attacking your mind, diluting your spirit of liberty.

Give yourself the confidence by running to me, every time you are in need.

Complete the vision by uniting yourself to the Source of freedom - which is Me, and connect.

I love you and I will not see you neglected.

Listen to me; your day is not yet over, nor shall your life be controlled by the destroyer who is attacking your mind - telling you otherwise.

Escape the grip - therefore escape the agony of sorrow and what tomorrow may bring.

The day is not yet over; you have a way out. Take it and run for your life. This is your opportunity of escape - Take it.

Let Go

14

Climb Higher

The time has come for me to release blessings and benefits to you.

You are not captured, but very much raptured from the storms causing havoc in your midst.

Their nagging and constant friction to be fed is not of me, but of the evil one oppressing you with thoughts that are not real, but delusional.

You are not to give into them; rather stay away from them.

I am your All; you are not to live in misery and strife, but rather in the destiny of heaven calling you home to be with me - free from all addiction.

Child, wake up from your injuring addiction causing you pain.

Oh, my beloved, the concert is now over, and the fruit of your hard work shall soon be seen.

15

Be Anchored

Return to me with all your heart, and free yourself from these restrictions tormenting you day-in day-out, and live a life of love all day, every day, and in every way.

Be alert and smarten up, for your father had the same addiction as you. You saw what happened to him-- he died, passed away in sorrow, owed money and experienced gloom and doom; misfortune all the way through. You do not need to follow his steps of grief, rather give up on that which is hurting you and release yourself from agony, sorrow and sadness entangling your thoughts against Me.

Turn to me and away from disaster.

Your *will* should not be to survive sickness, but to be free from addiction.

Now... Now... Now... is the right time for you. Scream it out and say, "I'm done with you."

16

Disrupt Not

Be free, be ready to fly - I am your Deliverer of hearts, Savior of souls.

Accuse not your brother falsely, for he is in severe pain over this situation-- his addiction tormenting him with sorrow. This addiction is killing him slowly, causing confusion and condemnation-- leaving him feeling guilty; while destroying his soul. You are to endure his behavior for a time, until he is risen from the dead, and from death he shall rise again. I shall comfort him, but you must first love on him and care for him. He is the child of your mother, the very born of your father, and Me your God - the Savior of mankind.

Watch over yourself as well, for you are the apple of my eye before the eyes of all.

Turn to Me - your Healer, and redeem yourself through my forgiveness poured out on you. Keep safe from addiction.

17

Injure Not Yourself

Carry not the weight of this world upon your own shoulders burdening you; instead, cross over from death to life empowering you, and be free from any restriction holding you back from moving forward in my will to survive.

Be free from addictive spirits tricking your mind and messing with your head - telling you otherwise. These forms are not angelic beings supporting you, rather wickedness sent forth aimed to destroy you. With sweet seduction they try to influence you. Move away from them all and lead a free life enriching you.

Hold on tightly and never let go of my Spirit supporting you. In quietness and peace, turn to me and you will find rest for your weary soul, for this is a vicious cycle tormenting you.

Keep calm even if the storms are rising.

The key is in your hands. Run from affliction.

18

Be Set Free

Free yourself from this addiction, for it is not pleasing in my eyes to watch you cry all day, grieving all night.

Take hold of my life, that you may die to self, and gain a better life - The resurrected life.

Grieve no longer, for my purpose shall be fulfilled in the midst of all this darkness ruining your image of me.

The weapons of your warfare are at stake. Resist not my helping hand that comes to you through others-- from those who are and willing to support you.

I shall call you to walk away from every struggle suppressing your mind towards me.

Be not reluctant to move forward, and away with me from all this pressure attacking you.

I am yours for all eternity.

19

Believe in Yourself

Retrieve, look away from it all. Say goodbye to your addiction which is holding you back from moving forward. Do not be tortured by it any longer. Look not to your past for help, rather learn from your experiences of today instead. I tell you, "Throw away every confusing thing by replacing it with love, peace, and harmony."

The old is gone, and a new journey has just begun. I am the Alpha and the Omega of your beginning, till the very end of your life. Your future is here for all eternity.

You are my Sun that shines, O my God, Redeemer of my soul. To you I turn and lean on, for you are compassionate. My soul is grieving, especially at a time like this.

Keep calm, Oh, my child of grace, even if the storms were to hit other towns that are not your own, and let go of disillusionment.

20

Grow Strong

Clear yourself from addition before it ruins your life and leaves you with regret. You are to empower yourself over your own sorrows by running the race marked out for you with great diligence, and not allowing the destroyer of lives to capture you in your weakness.

You are to climb higher by soaring above the hills, the mountains and the deep valleys.

Let Love for self, speak louder than the temptation of addiction seducing you, and be captivated by the power within you to overcome every difficulty oppressing your spirit, and be restored to health.

I understand, child, that it has been hard on you in the last few years, and you couldn't resist the temptation of giving in, but now it is a new day, a new way of retrieving and pulling through, for I am with you always.

You are an overcomer.

21

You Are Empowered

Call on Me, for I am near. Cry out to me, to reach you.

The flowers shall blossom and the sun shall shine, just as my everlasting love for you shall never end, but will forever remain alive.

You are not held back by addiction any longer. Therefore, you need not suffer the consequence of guilt.

You are free to enjoy life for the rest of your journey here on earth with me.

Complete, it is now done. You are free to soar. Walk with freedom, release love in action and maneuver as you so now please.

You are not restricted by devastation. Prepared, you shall always be free to soar away with me - your Freedom.

The aim is to see you free in Me - Your Deliverer, the One you are to call upon.

22

Be Encouraged

Addiction is truly your enemy.

Why waste time on something that does not fulfil your purpose and ruin lives?

Complete your one and only desire to be free from addiction that you may be spared the agony of death.

Release your burdens by letting go from what once bound you and ruined you completely.

I am on your side to help you be set free, but you must also allow me to intervene and loosen you from all this corruptibility restraining your ability to let go.

Seduced you shall not always be.

I am your helper and I will not see you come to ruin, for you mean much to me, to see you sit in ruin and waste away to nothing.

You are an overcomer - be captivated by life.

23

Be Renewed

Addiction is a form of sickness entangling you. You are to run away from it and escape the grip of its horror-- whether be gambling, eating, drinking, sexual, or simply laziness; you are to get rid of the consistency of its drain hovering over your life. Keep calm and act on my Will to free you from pressure and release you from imprisonment.

Be kind to yourself and be released from these form of pressures-- entangling your mind, disturbing your spirit. The sun is about to shine over your face and the moon shine over your head. So now keep warm and rested, for you are about to be free.

Climb the mountains without any form of restrictions holding you back and be free from these tormenting times you had to go through and endure. I love you, child; you are not neglected; so now do not neglect yourself. You are love beyond measure.

24

Be Lifted Up

Say help me God, and I will turn quickly to support you and will not keep you in ruin, for you have proved faithful by calling my name and I do hear and listen to the cry of the needy who are in desperate in need of me in their lives calling me.

You needed me once before and I looked after you, now ask me again and I will turn and lead you the Way of Truth in the direction best chosen for you by grace.

You will not be neglected, for I the One who loves you, and am He who will not see you lack any help that you seek.

You shall complete your journey in full health, and will master your freedom by me helping you achieve the success needed for you to be completely free from this addiction ruining your mind, deforming your spirit without me.

 I shall help you and you will be set free.

25

Joy In Freedom

Be empowered child, you are not alone in this journey of frustration and ruin.

I have beheld you since your youth and will not see you come to ruin, for your addictive nature is not in control of you, but rather I am. I will not let you miss out on anything of value without first giving a warning to repent and readjust your way of thinking to my way of love and freedom.

Do not ruin your life by complications, but rather, release yourself and be released to recover the journey. Be empowered and know that I am with you forever more.

You shall know the truth by the love you have inside you, which can free you from all these hardships you are going through by yourself without anyone supporting you; but I am on your side and will complete your journey lavishly.

26

Agony Gone

Wake O Child of mine, wake up and know that I am with you body, soul and spirit. Know my Will and walk with freedom in the direction chosen for you by grace, which I have accomplished on your behalf and for you, so that you will not come to ruin.

I have watched your ways and considered the cost, so that you may know how to handle your situation overtaking you.

I love those who love me, and enjoy setting them free, and those who have not heard of me yet, will also be blessed by knowing me through your freedom as a testimony given to them by my love setting you free.

Call on me and give me the upper hand on your addiction by empowering to let it go and let me in.

I love you, and I will support you by the love you share and give to yourself from me.

27

Benefit Thy Self

Addictions ruin lives; have nothing to do with its claws, for it is a very dangerous weapon tormenting you.

I need you to be strong, so that you may overcome every difficulty and trial facing you, coming from this addiction that has held you by the throat for years now… Let it go and run away from it, for it is not doing you any good, but only harm bringing you.

Let it go, let it not ruin your life.

Reflect on what I am saying, and heal yourself from all this trouble caused by your addiction to give into its substances injuring you.

Be empowered by love instead, that you may know the difference, and escape the grip of the fowler holding you captive by his stripes attacking your mind; stripping you naked and weighing you down by all sorts of difficulties.

A Prayer

From The Heart

Touch Me

O God, may I come out of this addiction draining my brain and ruining me in sorrow and affliction.

Help recover the loss this addiction has caused to my family financially, and the severe pressure it has put on me.

Recover me I pray, and allow it not to hold me captive, for I am in need of you to recover and restore the loss it has cost me in every way.

Revive me once again that I may see the sun and walk in your light of life I ask, for I no longer can take the torment this addiction is causing me.

I pray for a free life from all this sorrow, that I put myself in by given into these temptations now oppressing me.

Help me, I pray, that I may recover the loss and be found in you.

Restore Me

Thank you, God, for relief from all these addictions that once controlled my life by the spirit of negativity.

I am relying on you to free me completely, now that I know better.

I pray for the healing of my spirit, soul, body and mind, and offer myself to you completely by the power of love supporting me.

I your servant am relying on you to set me free, from all these burdens capturing my thoughts, entangling my mind, and dissolving me - bringing me to no good end.

I need you by my side to see me through all my difficulties surrounding me.

I need you more than ever and from all these afflictions to set me free.

Help me be free, Oh, my God of Love.

Rest Me

O God of hearts, heal my broken heart from all these afflictions ruining my mind and tearing me to pieces.

I do not know which way to go, nor to turn, but only to you I call and find satisfaction.

I am in ruin because of my addictive nature which has destroyed every good thing in my life and brought destruction upon my family, friends, neighbors and everyone that I could have helped instead.

Capture my heart that I may master my mind and ruin all that is trying to ruin me, by overcoming every difficulty that I face by your good spirit leading me.

Help me surrender to you and grow to know you better.

May I find joy in running into your arms of love and satisfaction healing me.

> # Enjoy Your Freedom
> *I Am With You*

★ *1 Jn 5:4* **for everyone born of God overcomes the world. This is the victory that has overcome the world, even our faith.**

Psa 108:13 **With God we will gain the victory, and he will trample down our enemies.**

Psa 68:19 **Praise be to the Lord, to God our Savior, who daily bears our burdens.**

You Are Free From Bondage
Seek Me

★ *1 Cor 16:13* **Be on your guard; stand firm in the faith; be courageous; be strong.**

Psa 129:2 **"they have greatly oppressed me from my youth, but they have not gained the victory over me.**

Psa 44:7 **but you give us victory over our enemies, you put our adversaries to shame.**

A NEW BEGINNING

A NEW JOURNEY

Check out our range of exciting and motivational new **B**eyond **W**oman® books, inspirational music, irresistible fragrance and selection of empowering products!

www.MyBeyondWoman.com

facebook.com/AuthorLinaM

facebook.com/BeyondWoman

facebook.com/MyBeyondWoman

twitter.com/MyBeyondWoman

instagram.com/MyBeyondWoman

youtube.com/MyBeyondWoman

www.ingramcontent.com/pod-product-compliance
Lightning Source LLC
Chambersburg PA
CBHW070550300426
44113CB00011B/1857